# BEYOND HERE
*and Other Poems*

# BEYOND HERE
## *and Other Poems*

Bishnupada Sethi

HAR-ANAND
PUBLICATIONS PVT LTD

To

Vaishali, Mahima & Alekh

HAR-ANAND PUBLICATIONS PVT LTD
E-49/3, Okhla Industrial Area, Phase-II, New Delhi-110020
Tel.: 41603490
E-mail: info@haranandbooks.com/haranand@rediffmail.com
Shop online at: www.haranandbooks.com



Published by Ashok Gosain and Ashish Gosain for
Har-Anand Publications Pvt Ltd

Printed in India at Aakash Press.

# Preface

Bishnupada Sethi brings into his Poetry an amazing range of concerns, unaffected by the contemporary slideshow of contemporary modernity. He shuns the imitative penchant for syntax-breaking modernity that has mindlessly reduced the fine art of Poetry into a mimicry of sorts. Bishnupada's Poetry is the Poetry of substance. This, infact, is the crux of a raging debate in creative writing steadfastly kept alive by pompous stylists who advance the theory that a poem need have no substance. This is where the poetic utterances of *Beyond Here* quietly intervene to make a point about the performativity of Poetry as a life-sustaining exercise. This particularly is the matrix in which an Indian Poet operates undaunted by the pressing panorama of multiple Englishnesses that pass off as the diction of English Poetry. English, for Indians is an Indian Language, and mercifully without the colonial tag any longer. Bishnupada, is an Odia-Indian who writes in English as he would write in his mother tongue Odia, a classical language of India. That brings into his Poetry a civilizational vision, unavailable to many modern languages. He writes about his home, about his Indian identity and about his engagement with the Universal, without any conceit, guile or ruse. Here is a genuine Poet in conversation with the many levels of his being, while the deep structure of his reality is embedded in brooding metaphysics 'beyond here.'

**Haraprasad Das**

# Contents

# A Fulfilling Sense

Under the clear open sky
While countless stars gazed quietly
And were pouring their energy kindly
In the midst of unknown people
Unmindful of others' existence
We met as two breathing shadows.

Two heated minds
Both the charged bodies
Talked in the ancient language
Of intimate bonding.

The story had begun
At first of our meetings.
A timeless hidden spark was in the waiting
Till then to ignite.

Two homeless wandering souls
Separated by the long spell of time
Place and birth
Fell for each other
At their first sight.

No one will name this story ever
As we couldn't be writing anywhere.
The love will simply evaporate in the air
Like the dews on the green leaves
And the cover of night's darkness
And our footprints in the avenue.

We live with our feelings
The most precious treasures hidden inside.
The fervour of our love is a fulfilling sense.
It prompts a perpetual smile on our lips.
The eye winks uncover
The beautiful islands of our hearts
Only discovered by both of us.

# A Lone Traveler

Where did my path begin
I can't remember.
Where am I going finally
Not so sure.
Few portions of my journey
Though still vivid
Many others have disappeared
From my memory.

The route was not linear always
Difficult and tough at times.
Light and darkness
Dreams and despair
Played a game
Of hide and seek
Making the path both
Easy and difficult.

I wonder at times-
Why at all this journey
And someone says-
I have been ordained to travel

Like planets and astral bodies
I have started from a point
Of space and time.
Towards the end of journey
As my strength wears out
The road tapers.

No one was known before who-
Joined me at many points of life
And identified by names,
Claimed some relations
And left my company later
While some others still remain.

The process of joining
And leaving me
Continues throughout.
It makes me feel
I'm a lonely being-
I carry my own baggage,
None was with me,
None will accompany,
For all the time or forever.

# Ageless Portrait

Each time I look at the portrait,
It appears ageless.
The attachment grows.
I get drawn to nostalgia-
A series of life events
That brought two souls closer
Culminating though rituals
For establishing stronger bonds
As we got new identities,
That moment is frozen.

I see the excitement
About a new beginning
Of a journey of togetherness
Lurking in our eyes.

The glimpses flash before me-
The solemn air
Hymns, flowers
Sacred fire, prayers and priest
Hall teeming with guests, relatives
Best wishes, blessings and gratitude

Mixed with anxieties and expectations
As a new phase was unfolding.

In hindsight-
I'm led to believe
Nothing else would have been possible.
The path from past to the present
And the way forward too-
Looks charted out.

# Ahimsa

I can hear the soft voice-
'Hey Ram! '
It was just like Jesus uttering-
"Father, forgive them, for they do not know what they are doing"
Everyday
As I cross many junctions in life.

One would wonder
How could He bless
When the fragile body
Felt the most acute pain
And turned lifeless in minutes!

The ubiquitous is his name.
A splendid work the followers did
To keep the glorious memories
Of universal values and morals alive
Till our civilizations last.

Each word he spoke,
Each action he displayed

Gave rocklike strength where upon-
We build on our dreams.

Decades later we wonder
If it wasn't a miracle
He walked around here
Being in flesh and blood!
So tall and big was he
Within his embrace
Came the entire world.

A life, a message
Of ever expanding love.
Ahmisa is the realm
Of consciousness.
A true scientist he was
Always experimenting with
Infinite capacity to love.
There was boundless joy
In all his trials and storms.

Keeping himself quite light
He walked tall.
To all those following behind
He was a sage.
His soul and body were different.
Like a horse before the cart
He was pulling his body.
All his followers are worthy creations
Of God, people worship

In different forms.
He saw no caste, no creed
No colour, no sex.

He was a mystery
As he knew
Thousand years before-
There is enough for everyone
To meet the needs on earth.
There is hardly any necessity to seek
Protection from another human being
And that is possible only if
People adopted-
'Ahimsa' – as a principle
Of unifying force
For the humanity to survive
In this cosmos
So unfathomable.

# As I Draw a Deep Breath

A few decades ago
I was a child and I remember-
How I woke up early in the morning
To the lament singing
Of a group of women
In the neighbour's house
As a female calf had died there.
While sobbing badly
They were heaping all praises
Upon the dead animal
For its innocence and beautiful manners
And they were praying
To help it move
From this world to another
To the land of dead
And further
By way of rebirth
And all happier times.

On our way to the village school
There existed a vast meadow.
While passing by

The children would often sprint
A few hundred meters
To escape the stench in the air.

From a little distance
It would appear –
As if a few old ladies
Covering themselves with umbrellas
Made of palm leaves
Were quietly collecting
Fish from the flowing rain waters.

Such was the sight of large birds
Quietly guarding the prey,
While the dogs and jackals would wait
Being pushed further away.

A large number of tiger spirited
Black vultures
Soared and floated in circles
Over the meadow.

They would sense their food.
While descending down
With all their might
They would tuck into the meal,
The bald head and neck
Making it easy
My village was their temporary abode.

Now the old world is gone,
So also the tradition of lament singing-
As the modern time frowned upon it.
The vultures are gone.
And gone are the carcasses.

At this time-
When the world is locked down
A gloom has descended,
A fear gripped us all.

Believe me
As I draw a deep breath,
A smell of familiar stench-
Unnerves me.

Someone is dying.
Some are in acute pain.
There is no one to do a favour-
By lament singing.

# As the Time Gallops Away

When I look around I notice
Few decades have simply rolled by-
As if it was only yesterday
Everything happened in my life
For the first time
And its memory remains fresh.

Standing in the front
Of a thousand year old temple,
A splendid spectacle of human glory,
A witness to the changing times,
I piece a thread through our humanity
And a certain pride fills in me-
How lucky a descendant of a great race
That have I been!

I can hardly comprehend
How vast is the nature of Time!
Insignificant is my space-
I can comprehend only
A bit of our universe.

We didn't know each other
Till we came across in our lives.
Beyond a certain time we know
We will cease to exist.

My heart becomes very heavy
To realize this truth-
We are sure of never meeting again
In the same bodies and consciousness
Never know of anything beyond
Our last moments on the earth
While the clock would still be ticking away.

Let's realize the limitations of our spaces
And catch up with the speed of Time,
Drop what we don't carry,
Letting all thoughts of repentance go,
Making easy our hard feelings,
In this beautiful universe
There's nothing more important
Than the time of togetherness
We have at our disposal.

# Ashes, Charcoal and Identities

There is chill
More in the air than usual.
The night appeared heavier.
Though the nearby landmass was duty bound
To cool the heated sea
But the rule here is broken.
The gush of sea breeze
Blows over the heaps of blazing wooden logs.

The sands have darkened, where
I searched for the dreams of my ancestors
Within those fine charcoals
And the moisture in the air.

We carried here last of his things
Including the silent body he possessed.
Nothing will be taken back from here
Except few confusing beliefs
And fond memories.

I looked back
For the last time

As I prepared to leave.
The sky above,
The thundering sea,
The forgetful mortal beings
Hardly gave a convincing reason
To believe-
If I were anything or
What I claim myself to be.

Few more wailing people join
Crowding the place.
The focus of attention changes place.
No one asks and remembers-
Who came,
Who went away.
The identity is reduced to
Mere ashes,
Few charcoal
Without the names-
All lie scattered.

# At the End

At the end
It's now some memories-
Of pain and pleasure.
You walked away
As it was so easy for you.

In this freezing winter night
I have put up a happy face
And stand before all
Pretending to be fine.
Yonder I see few walls
In places I thought
To build bridges over.

What do I say about?
How do I remember you
For the pains
Or pleasure I received?

Yet I claim my victory-
You are now gone.
I am there past mid night
I will welcome the new Sun.

# Before You Walk Away

It's a storm, very rare-
Hear from the ocean it's roars
Rising from deep inside while
Tall trees are swinging in the air
The objects are flying hither-tither.

The nests birds'd made are gone.
Nothing as it appears will remain-
End of the world nearing
The feeble hearted was heard saying.

Look at that little girl
In the hut of a wise farmer
Trying to save the lamp glowing
Providing a hand cover in the house corner.
Dispelling darkness away
She's quite aware of the storm's power.

Look back before you leave if you must
Think of giving love chance another.
No storm will last forever.
What you do now will decide the future.

However hard you may try
None could run the clock backwards.
Neither will you be young again
Nor your fresh beginnings can
Recreate the same innocent feelings
To pour all over your life's spaces.

You may hold back to what you have now.
Lying low is little wise, at times, not so bad.
How do we look at a burnt limb of body
If one're to live with it!

Before all old memories are blackened
And you walked out of the problems now
You may give love another chance
And allow the healings
To start to cover the wounds
As the storm blows over.

# Beyond the Lock Down

Do not ask someone else-
How much it hurts
When one feels the pain
Due to hunger or bad times!

Not a day or weeks few-
All belongings I possess
I carry.
My feet give me the strength,
The head and shoulder support.
My family and I
Move miles and miles
Over the years
In search of work, food and rest.
Not sure if I remember
The year and month.

Sunrise and sunset guide my day-
I continue the journey
Unmindful of cyclone and flood
Drought and epidemic drive me further away.

My feet are bared.
Little clothes I do wear.
Heat, rain and cold
All the extreme weather
Hurt me and benumb.

I rise to go-
The earth below
And the sky above
Give me a call
And fill my mind with strength
My dear ones need to smile and grow.

# Beyond that Time

Of imperfections
Of unsatisfying deeds
Of short lasting glories
Of feeble desires
Of umpteen worries
Of limited time and space
Of senseless races-
Are our lives' stories.

They will judge you
Nevertheless-
Though not praising you for all good deeds,
Not many are taking notes
Of all omissions.

A little away
There is seated a sage
Forsaking the best things he could have had.
His eyes are lotus shaped,
Cryptic are his smiles.

One would wonder
If winter would touch his bare body

Whether the scornful conduct
Of the alms giver would ever hurt him!

What does more he know?
Does he observe anything
Beyond that time
We don't count?

# Cheering up the Brave Hearts

Faith is shaken-
Each human being poses
A perceived threat to the other,
Not being an enemy.

A known enemy
But invisible
Traveled worldwide using
Human body as the medium.
Victims are the self,
The loved family members,
Kith and kin,
The neighborhood and
Unknown yet harmless people around.

Much has changed
In only few months,
The rich and mighty too hit very badly-
Untold miseries have surfaced.

Exposed to the maximum risk
The brave medicos and paramedics

Have taken the battle heads on-
At this trying times of human history.

We stand to cheer up the brave hearts.
They remind-
Like many a times in the past
As a human civilization
We shall have the conquest
With science as a weapon.

# Clueless

Mid in the night
When none was around
The silence was ruling absolutely
And my door was closed.

I felt I was struggling to escape
As I had been held by someone very tight.
My body had a feeling, stone like.
I needed to breathe.
Despite my last efforts to wriggle out
He didn't let me go.
Only I wished if there was someone
Who could rush in to help me out
But I could hardly shout.

Shivering and sweating
With very high pulse rate
I was waiting to see
If my end was nearing
While suddenly I could rise up
To find none around
I was lying cool.
Certain eerie emptiness was only prevailing.

What was it?
Who was he?
Could it be real?
Powerful no less than a monster
Or a ghost I had been longing to see!

Or is it my accumulated fear
Hidden somewhere deep inside.
What could my fear be-
Loss of loved ones?
Loss of job, food, other basics?
Loss of honour, esteem, freedom?
Loss of youth, health or life
Or something very valued
I am not aware of
Though I lose something everyday.

I ponder-
What could be my status at that time
When I become nothing
With no body, no name
Completely reduced beyond ashes.
There'll be nothing to shed.
Whether I'll still fear from something

I am clueless
As I was deeply asleep
A while ago
Still I was in some noose
Not being in the control of my body.

# On Daughter's Day

It was a music
Soft and subtle,
The early morning rains sang
To the tunes of gentle breeze
While the humming bees added rhymes.
A celestial fragrance was wafting all around
To the charms of drifting clouds.
The sky was overcast.
The Sun rays were peeping in
From behind.
A stage was set
For someone to arrive.

It has been since then
The non stop music-
Quite an essence of my life
Being played ceaselessly.
I draw inspiration-
How is someone
So little yet so wise!
She judges-
What I should do

And should not.
In the difficult moments
She comes in between
Like a shield
The trouble and me-
So soft and yet so strong
Like the silk threads.
She exerts an influence-
As one needs air
So she is there.

How lucky
Have I been
To have a daughter
Lively and pretty!
She is a blessing
From the heavens-
Cheering all the way
And making a life so full.

# Do not Pull the Trigger

Stop
Don't pull the trigger.

Look
At the tiny feet and hands
Hazel shaped eyes popping out
From beneath the desks.

Your boots scare
More than the cockroaches and rodents
They have ever dared.

See the school bags
Books, pencils, chalks and snack boxes
All scattered around.
They have come here to know
More about the world
Allah has created.
They know not
Who is a friend
And if there is an enemy.

I wish you knew a child
And ever played with him.
Remember if you saw
Hidden something
Behind the smiles and feelings
A truly divine innocence.

Don't pull the trigger
Don't silence the laughter.

# Feeling Ecstatic

There is profusion of light.
The heat and cold are absent.
I don't feel any need to see through the eyes.
My body and limbs are dissolved.
I don't hear any voice.
I lost my speech,
My hunger and thirst.
These senses are no more required-
And have gone dumb.
I don't need to breathe.

Fire won't burn me anymore.
Storms don't blow me away.
Mighty ocean does hardly scare.
No sharp object could pierce into me.
No force could harm me again.
I have risen above all such pain.

I am nameless.
I have no form.

There is an ecstasy
In the complete absence of any pain.
All over I am overpowered.
A bountiful joy surrounds.
I keep flying over-
Here, there and everywhere,
Over a unique dimension,
The past, present and future merge together.

# Final Ordeal

Why is this ordeal
I have to pass
By jumping into the fire
And come out unscathed
And you stand out
Quiet over there?

It's not the first time
I was asked for a test.
In fact I have to qualify
How I talk
How I walk
How I live
And what others think of me
Every moment.

Living as per certain principles
Is definitely what I do-
Still I dislike these tests
Time and again.
You want me-
I should come perfect

In front of the whole world
Then you could accept me

I've my agonies-
You are yet to know me fully.
A conflicting battle,
A silent revolt wages within
My body and mind wither,
I withstand till a threshold

This is my final ordeal
I wish to defy.
I've decided to assert.
Between the narrow divides of the earth
I've negotiated a path.
I shall be free
And settle on my own terms.

# Fire Within

From toe to the head
And everywhere from within
A sensation and acute pain is felt
I'm burning
And not known since when
The process started.
I make another attempt
To pacify the mind
To douse the ravaging fire.

The smoke billows out
Reaching far and wide
A layer of another cloud is formed
Everything looks hazy.

How old is the fire
Till when would it rage
Will I be charred and ground
Beyond any recognition.

The fire will satisfy itself
I'm no more anything
Even the ash particles will blow away
I'll not be there
As I didn't exist.

# For a Bereaved Mother

He can hide behind the darkness.
He can merge within the light rays.
He can take any hue of the tree leaves.
May it be any colour of the sky
Or the ocean
To match with their pigments
Is no issue with him now.

You knew him so much.
It did matter a little
Whether he was here and there
And so familiar were you
With his contours.

You are the greatest artist ever known.
You created him,
Sustained him all throughout
From the time
He was only an egg
Till he grew up so big.

Now you can take a pen,
Use the sky or the ocean,

Shade of darkness
Or the patch of light rays
Or the tree trunk
Or any empty space
As a canvas
Draw him as you wish-
A toddler
A teenager
An adult in prime youth
Or any form you remember.

Feel him
He is here
On the clouds
In the sky
On the ocean
On the tree tops
Over the hills and meadows
And wherever reaches
Your eyes and mind.

He was here and there
Now, he is everywhere.

# From Inside a Room of Life

What that is
Connecting a real world
Of material and senses
To another realm
Of unknowns?

The living energy-
Does it ever come to a halt?
Can that be extinguished
Or dissipated?

Surely it can't be destroyed.
It has to exist somewhere
In the same or another form
And there should be a doorway
Connecting this real world-
Quite theatrical though
And still appearing permanent
Through certain illusion and rules,
To another one-
Beyond our scope.

From inside a room of life,
Strongly enclosed
Within the most opaque wall
As we seek to peep out
Nothing of our abilities
Comes to help.

While we living beings
Experience and extrapolate,
A vast and limitless universe
Of space, matter
Time and energy,
We fail to comprehend-
How that only thing
Which makes you feel exist
Vanish once for all
Leaving no discreet link?

# Garland in My Cupboard

I was just thinking about you-
Unmindful while walking in the garden.
The fragrance of jasmine awakened me
As if someone poured over a bucketful of dew.
I felt very cool and fresh
All over my body and mind.

I was drawn back to those days
You weren't in my life then
Yet certain closeness was developing.
So many random words
Sweet sensations, dreams and plans
Flew in the air
Filling every space of daily chores.

Each of the days in waiting
Passed like a year.
It's simply not a pain
Of not being with you
But a feeling of how our coming together
New excitement and great happiness
Kept the division between days and nights away.

Golden moments and cherished events
Came with the blessings from all over.
We became one and felt as if-
We had been separated earlier
To be reunited again.

Each of your temporary absences
Gave immense pain.
Nothing was pleasant on earth,
Sleep and easiness eluded
When you were not there.

I laugh at many of our stupidities
Including when the cop had reprimanded
For certain innocent public acts
And things others didn't like.
Certain craziness for you kept me alive
Through the thick and thin of tumultuous life.

I must admit-
Though everything didn't come
As a blessing to our lives,
Yet I recount all the beautiful moments,
Each of those a jasmine flower that you like,
I am making a beautiful garland
And hiding in my cupboard
With a request if you could
Place on me
While I take up the life's last journey.

# Give Me My Bicycle

Give me back
My bicycle-
The one I had
For the first time
In my childhood.

It was in a moonlit night
When the most precious
Of my possessions
I brought from the market.
All throughout the route
Tried to ride in phases
Wherever I could.

The whole night-
I was half awoke
Getting up in between
Time and again.
That it was right there
Chained to the pillar.

Morning came earlier
Than the usual time
The next day
And I was on the serpentine road
Of my village.
I could move faster
Up and down
Effortlessly
Without touching the soil,
Beat anyone who're on foot.
In a while I'd made rounds
Of the world that was mine.

Not that I didn't know-
My bicycle had no life.
Yet I took its care
Like one does
For one's child.

Decades have passed since-
I search for my bicycle
Or any other thing in life
That gave so much
Excitements and joy.

# Glowing in Self-love

An intense and fiery relationship
Once anchored on firm grounds
Of mutual love and respect
Looked for a shared future
Became a subject of envy too.
Few drew parallels  from lores
Saying how again two separated souls
Got together in this life.

It'll be untrue to say
There weren't lows in life.
During the times storms blew over
The bonds became weak,
Yet I made efforts
To be back in life's routine.

As an ordinary mortal however
With finite strength
I experience today
The weakest point in life-
No more desire is there to make another effort

To hold back or reverse the time
To be upset or angry

And to enter the never ending cycle
Of affection and bitterness
Of lows and highs.

The thinning of bonds
Forces me to look within-
To discover I've no fear,
Immense source of soul force lies
Hitherto untapped
Blemish free, never hurting
Unhindered and unconditional.

I glow in self love
Feeling unfettered
And cared for.
I'm loveable eternally.

# He Came Out of the Temple

Lord of the universe
Following an age old tradition
Rode on a huge chariot
Covered with red and yellow canopy
On the grand avenue
Accompanied by His siblings separately
To bestow blessings on the mortals
And fulfill their wishes
To the chant of His holy names
And the music made by drum beats, conch and cymbals.

The grand spectacle is viewed
By everyone in the universe
And by the gods and goddesses
From up in the heaven.

Human beings fail to see-
How numerous souls
Ghostly bodies too
Wander near the chariots
And trail behind

Waiting for that particular moment
On return from the sojourn.

Barrels of holy drinks in earthen pitchers
Made of rich ingredients
After those are offered to the deities
As a ritual get smashed
Spilling all over
On the floors of chariots.

Numerous spirits, souls
And entities of other world
After waiting for a year or more
Compete with each other
Like the human devotees
To get a little of the potion
In their efforts to attain salvation.

He came out of the temple.
No one could stop Him.
He had reasons-
Few stated and many unknowns.

# He Exists

I was feeling hurt
Bullied, desolate and bereft-
Sobbingly, I looked out
For those firm hands,
A masterly voice
And for drawing solace.

Travelling bare feet
Withstanding hot sand and Sun
Before I could give up
He would lift me on his shoulder,
The mightiest and strongest of the men-
I would've nothing to fear.

Many of the storms I weathered
Hardly left a scratch mark-
I saw the nature's fury
Ravishing everything
Ruining man's pride.
Yet I had sound sleep
No worry in the mind.

I don't remember any great pain I'd
Of hunger, thirst or fever.
The stout hands cared-
The love was unconditional
Enveloping my world.

Decades later, now
Upon hearing something unpleasant
Or at irregular times
I would hear the same voice feeble though-
"There's nothing to worry my son
For there's God
He has His hands upon you
Like I held your hands once
And He knows His job well.
Never to feel low
Or let down
Have your faith on Him
Trust me He exists
Nothing could be there
Without His wish."

# Here is a Message

There is certain silence in the air
Broken by the incessant rain drops
On the roof tops and the tree branches.
The coolness wafted by the breeze
Doesn't rupture the silence in the hall.

The music of rain goes on
In perfect rhymes and volume.
The voices here have gone mute.
The focus of attention drifts
From the music of nature around
To the celebrations and events
Of the past.

Why do untimely events take place?
Why did the dark clouds descend
When the Sun blazed
The day being at the peak of brightness?

Here is a message
Deep down from the fresh memory-
You are in your deep slumber.

Everything remains as it was before.
Believe in the past being real
As much as you trust your present.
He was there.
He is there.
Don't trust so much the current turn of events
To disbelieve in the past.
In this realm
The past, present and future coalesce
And the time is not linear.
You can move from your place to anywhere.
You could be there
Anywhere and everywhere.

# I'm Superb, I'm Beautiful

My soul struggles
In the trappings of a coloured skin.
Often as I look at my face
In the mirror
My inner fear compounds.
I would face the same unkind people
And hear their hateful comments
From near my ears loud-
I'm nothing and I'm no good.

Several of the questions
Scald my skin
Rip my identity.
I've discovered
Many years of acquaintances
Hid plenty of lies and deceptions.
My tarnished soul
Struggles to run free.

Those words act like whiplashes.
My feet falter.
Blood and tears drip

Inside my mind and soul.
The raging of a battle inside
Seeks time for a quick end.

But I realised-
No one had forced
To accept a sort of slavery
Though years' of conditioning
Gave a false sense
Of beauty and wit
That the other side was blessed with.

I will drop now
My own pretensions.
How could the merciful God
The most perfect being
Who instilled a kind life stream in me
Ever make anything ugly!

I'm no less
Than being superb
And the most beautiful!

# I have become Immortal

You may yet to know that-
Your lips are poetry.
Telling a fine story
It weaves a suave dream for me,
I wanted to tell all the time.

Deep in emotion
It stirs strong waves in me.
Elegantly poised
It heightens my desires
To set all bondages free.

Calling it luscious
Or most ravishing or matchless
Would hardly be proper and just
Since it lifts me higher
From an ordinary state.
The minds are melted together
The lips locked and
The quiet music of two beating hearts
Bares the souls
From all wrappings-
I become immortal.

# I Need a Portrait

I need a portrait-
You may wonder why?

Deep in the night hours
My thoughts
Rebound on the walls,
I wish to cross over.

The space inside
Is far too limited.
So also the life sustaining air
Which I might run out of.

Here are the bruises,
Abundance of senseless vacuum.
The wounds are unlikely
To ever be healed.

I need your portrait
To have a glance,
To gather strength and courage
To cross over all the walls,

To connect my past with the future,
To see the light rays of dawn tomorrow,
To witness the washing of rose petals
Of the garden by the night's dews.

The promises
The dreams in those eyes say-
Life isn't yet over,
The beauty is to be alive,
Only the living ones are beautiful
The rest are unknowns.

# I Wish to Know

I am sure-
I know
I don't belong to this place.
With the passage of time
I will be gone
As if I weren't there before.

How about those who know me?
They will also be gone
Like many others who left earlier.
New comers will fill up the space.
There may be someone
Or something
Connecting over the time and space
Making things appear permanent.

I encounter
The dead walls of thoughts
And suffocate
Being confined to my limited earthly space.
I stretch my memory
Backwards and forwards-

My existence is very frail.
Beyond my consciousness yet,
Events go on
Appearing disorderly though
Over a small fraction of time
And yet-
Following a perfect order
Over a longer time frame.

I wish to know
How do I connect
To the places and people
After I am gone!

# Beyond Here

I often wish to return
To the darkness where-
My shape disappears.

At the best
My faint shadowy
And wavering figure may show up
Immersed in unknown grooves
To the joy of an interplay
Of light and darkness.

The deeper breaths,
Wordless corporal communications,
Faster sensuous movement
Up and down
In the veins
Create a temporary sensation
I am alive
Deep here.

Beyond here-
In contrast

The world of dead lie entrenched
Well decorated with falsities
The legal relationships drive it
Under the glowing lampposts.

I belong to the starkest darkness
Where I'm dissolved.
I don't appear in a body.
No one judges me ugly.
I'm loved.
I'm eternal.
I'm in a blissful state.

# Just a Walk Away

How do you feel
When almost everyday
You hear someone you knew,
Lived together at some time
Or grew up with
Is no more?

At the beginning
Occasional were such events
Or the persons were not so close.
Feeble were the impressions
And hard feelings were very few.
Life was to go on
As long as the near ones
Stayed close
Or remained safe.

Now like the mushrooms
Of dark clouds of a fierce monsoon
The vultures of death
Lift one by one
Indiscriminately wherever you look.

Another friend is gone
And you ponder.
Does it indicate
If my time too is up?

Now I feel existing
Like a corpse.
A wall of mist
Is only separating two worlds
Of living
And the dead
And my shifting to the other side
Seems just a walk away.

# Keep Singing

Keep singing
My nightingale.
For this life is a song
And you sing so well.

When you sing
Many listen to the lyrics and rhythm.
I feel mesmerized.
The voice pierces my heart's ear.

A butterfly runs amok
Through these vibrations.
It runs here and there.
The soul seeks a passage
To escape the barriers
Of time and relationships,
Asks for a new definition of life
Its purposes.

The song is life.
The life is a song.

You are the lyrics
A beautiful mother wrote
And who inspired
To live a wonderful life.

# Let Some of the Desires

Let some of our desires-
Still remain as such
Like the fires wrapped
In the finest silken clothes.

There will be certain pains.
Some parts of us will burn-
Slowly but incessantly.
There will be never ending restlessness.
But all the discomfiture-
Will provide the fuel to our souls
To keep us on track
To drive us ahead.

Let us wait-
Till all our attractions wither away-
Nothing of us is left behind
To take any pride in it.

Just two beings remain
All bared.
The souls meet.
A timeless thirst is quenched.

# Life as Usual

I bow down to thank
The God of death
For relieving her
Of all the agonies.

She had been reduced
Merely to a frail body.
The memories were gone-
She didn't know who she was.
Something was forcing her to only cry.
Everything around her had lost their identities.

No less than a child she was-
Yet none wished her well being.
Her existence didn't inspire hopes,
She was no more useful to them
She had nourished with love and care.

I paused to reminisce-
It was in a late winter evening
Of my childhood days, years ago

During one of my visits to her home,
I was seated by her,
The heat of the hearth kept us warm.
A child wouldn't know-
What had kept thousands of people then hungry.
A despair had engulfed-
There was no work and job,
The crop had failed
All around existed-
A subdued and eerie silence.

She was making breads
Fresh and warm from ovens.
There was limited hunger in me,
She won't mind giving those
One by one as being made
Till the last grain of flour lasted.

I won't know
Till many years later
She had no food that night for her,
All others too remained hungry.
There was nothing left-
Only few ounces of food weren't enough
And what inhibited her
From sharing with everybody
Whatever was there!

The sky above is clear and bright today.
A certain emptiness I find in the silence

That rules around.
I won't find any answer
To whatever query I may have-
Yet its life as usual.

# Life is the Greatest Gift

Life is the greatest gift I got-
Unattached to any condition.
Being in the flesh and blood
And in senses-
To me is a boon of heaven.

Let's all gather
In the moment of this hour's celebration.
The glory of living resonates here
In the smell of our sweats
In those care and touch.
The hugs melt us.

I wouldn't mourn.
I won't remember the dark moments.
My tears didn't last long
Like the dark clouds
Which withered away soon.

I'm not in a hurry.
Why should I

When I can't stop the passage of time?
I will make the events I live through
Full of memories
Of cheers and laughter
With all shades of colours.

# Love is Around

You sat across
And talked mundane matters
While not noticing-
I was becoming restless.

I expected
To get few clues
How you valued our past-
In between what we talked.

Quite a lot of water
Seems to have been drained out
Since the high floods of our lives had
Washed us almost away
At very unusual times of our lives.

No promises were made then.
We didn't know the path forward.
Yet the hearts united-
Two minds thought alike.

Tracing and extrapolating,
Going back and forth,

Breathing in and out,
About a relationship so intimate
Gives beautiful earthly feelings.
Love is around.
It binds us together
Whether you speak about or not.
We exist.
We know each other.
We feel the love
In thought
In words
And in deep silences.

# Love Me or Leave Me

I wasn't very watchful
Being busy in things
That came on my way,
Then I realised
A year has gone by
As if it was only last night
We had welcomed a new year.
A fun filled event
Full of hugs and best wishes
Reminds the new expectations
Those came with a new Sun rise.

Since I wanted to be always better
The struggle had begun
Right after I gained consciousness.
The journey was gradual
And step by step
So engrossing was the movement
Through the time and space
That I didn't realise-
It has been few decades
I have moved ahead

From birth to youth
And still exist.
Introspecting today,
I realise the changes
That has occurred all around-
Who have all vanished?
How new faces have replaced the old guards?
My journey provides a lead
About the writing in bold
Which doesn't strike me often.

Being alive I can still feel
How the time and space
Are more infinite-
Than we comprehend.
Who hasn't been told
Soon it will get over.
There may not be a warning-
We will miss each other
The very next moment.

I have no clue to any existence
Beyond this living body
It may be only for few days
We are together-
Like my friends and masters were here
With or without a purpose
And their love and words
Bring fond memories.

Leave me or love me-
I'm unable to reserve
A time or space for any discord
That I don't fit into your needs.
I'm perfect the way I am-
No one loves me more
Than I love myself.
Where do I get the time
I'll give explanations
To seek your grace?

# Many Thousands Miles of Separation

We are just across
In the same house-
The wall which existed much before,
But you have really measured
Many thousands miles of our separation.

How the time changed so fast
Since when -
We thought our paths were converging
From a time when we'd met.
A mere sight of discomfort
Often I would love to feign though-
Drew so much of your attention.

We both thought
There could never be a time
We hardly could thrive alone!
A time of total darkness
We saw clouding
Even such a feeble thought!

Yet today I lie here-
Not being able to scare a fly
Ruling me all over-
I don't feel any hurt.

You are busy
Planning for a time beyond this-
As few more events are mere formalities
Soon to get over.

I don't exist,
You have to erase some memory.
Life is to be lived.
It was another period of your life
You have to forget
And you got to march ahead of it.

# I'm not Alone

Too weak hearted-
You screech to see me carry
The empty body of my beloved
On my shoulder.

Our Lord too-
Having gone wild
At the sight of His consort
Immersing in the sacrificial pyre
Moved about the universe
Carrying the mortal remains-
All for twelve years
Looking for someone
Who could revive Her
As none dared stop His Tandav
And He searched for
An immortal love
Till he dropped Her body parts
At all twelve places turned holy.

A rare privilege this is-
An intimate tribute

To someone I love
I'm carrying
Weighing a few pounds
Worn out due to earthly processes
On my hardened shoulder-
A bliss too difficult to describe.

Look at my face.
Am I complaining?
Though I'm sad
For losing my love,
I'm not in a hurry
To dispose of
What little remains as of now
Yet I search for her presence
Wherever I go.

The whispers of gentle breeze
The shadow of a tree,
The sound of a bird in the branches,
The wild flowers by the side of lanes,
The sight of knowns and unknowns
Remind that I am not alone.

# My Chase with the Monster

I was worried terribly-
I kept on running though.
The gap was closing
In between
As the monster was pursuing constantly.
His loud cries were deafening.

Sweating and palpitating
With prayers on the lips
I wasn't sure
If the chase would continue indefinitely
Or soon I'd falter
To be mauled over.
He would love to see
My blood stream dried out.

Am I still in sleep?
No more I'm sprinting.
No more worries disturb me.
I'm in a milieu of people
Known and many more unknown.
The hushed voice jostle

With the cool breeze blowing
From across the sea.
A sedate moon shines from the above
At this late night hours while
The monster lie on the ground.
His stern look gives a feel-
He is only in a deep sleep.
In a mixed feeling of beliefs and disbeliefs
I wonder as I gazed him
If my battle was over!

There's an inner voice
Wafting from all around-
It's time to give a quiet farewell
To the fear inside.
Life is a great gift.
Do good, be kind.
Monster would always be there
But won't rule over this earth-
It's the order.

# My Ego's Last Address

Countless and nameless birds
Rise up and go down
In perfect synchronization
At the sight of prey
And pure joy
In flocks
Leaving no trace of travelled trajectories
Near the shoreline
Into the azure blue sky
Resplendent with several tinges
Of multiple colors
Against a setting Sun.

Those don't live together,
Yet at this dusk hour
The groups are formed
In near perfect cohesion
As if preprogrammed
And controlled remotely.

A small sandy patch of land
Interspersed with half burnt charcoals-

A gateway to heaven they say it opens.
You can call it as human's last address
We will appear here for the last time.
The wailings of groups of people
Rise up and fall intermittently,
Reach quite far away from there.
Yet the regular watchman
Doesn't hear any of those,
Not getting irked by the fumes and smokes,
At times taking the comfort
From the heat in the fire.
He has been a witness
To all the rites
When ego, flesh and bones
Of small and big ones are charred.
The names are struck off
From all the directories thereafter.

# My Queries Rebound

The flickering lamp
And a limited zone around it
Sets my peripheries.
I'm at the mercy
Of the uncertain winds
And flow of unknown-
Yet finite amounts of energy.

Darkness exists
Beyond the reach of these rays.
It shall always be there-
Nothing ever shall push away
The same completely.

I'm handicapped.
All my senses are powerless
As those fail to reach
The time and space, where
I were there for certain.

Even more feeble become
All my comprehensions

And intelligible
At two points of life.

My queries rebound.
Everywhere I see a wall.
An obscure and steely darkness
Pervades around my existence.

# Nothing Unusual

Nothing unusual I see-
Though unexpected things happen.
The events have similarities to the past.
There are rules.
There is an order.
Beyond our consciousness
Things perpetuate.

Not yet known-
How many species
Observe the matter and lives
Beyond their limited senses?
We are bound
By the limits of a phenomenon
Called death.
The living ones miss
Some friends they once
Nudged together.
No one knows what's lying ahead
Beyond one's time.

The Sun will rise and set,
So also the moon without fail

There will be cycles of seasons.
The oceans and seas,
The streams and rivers,
The hills and forests-
Surely will exist beyond our times.
Unanswered will remain
Certain queries.
We will become numb
In the struggle for survival.
We will not seek meanings
The very next moment.

# On this Special Day

The breeze wafts around
The fragrance of burning incense sticks.
Underneath a solemn tree branch
From where too-
The sobs originate and rent the air.

There are freshly plucked bright flowers,
The resplendent vermilion marks,
The choicest sweets,
A glass of water-
Together these tell a story.

It's about life-
Of love,
Of togetherness,
Promises and trust-
A faith in the Supreme God.

She was told
She could protect her brother,
Get him a long life
By simply tying an amulet

On a special occasion once a year,
Who would promise her limitless love
Assure full protection and care.

Time could not be more cruel than to her today
As she is seated by a piece of stone,
Yet she believes-
Her bother is here around
And this is not a mere piece of stone
But a symbol of a timeless relationship.

They both need love and protection
Of each other.
The pain in her soul
And prayer in her tears
Connect each other-
Through cosmic powers.

# Our Names on the Sands of Time

The Sun was shining all over
Along the sea shore.
Unbearable was the heat
For our feet dipped in the soil.
The sea water kept us thirsty.
Still we walked together
Holding hand in hand
Wrote our names
On the sands of time.

Over the years-
We watched
How the winds blew
From the sea to the land
During the day time
And seawards after the evenings.

We witnessed
The calmness of winter,
The summer rage,
The storms of monsoon,

All the rules of nature
As two bystanders.

While the time has passed-
I still look for the traces
Of our names we wrote
On the sand bed of our prime
By connecting to the memories
I still have access to
And the rest part
To which all roads are now closed.

# Over the Time and Space

I'm here
Around you.
I'm there
Away from thee.
I'm above the ground
And on the floor by your side.

I'm here now
Like I'm there in the past.
Travelling from the past to future
And to the present
At random is so easy for me now.

I feel no pain.
I experience
No hunger no thirst
No anger no jealousy
No lust no greed
No remorse no sorrows
Having acquired different new senses.

I see you all sad
Though I know why.

I assure you
I'm too happy
Like I was never before.

I'm feeling elevation.
A sense of tremendous joy
Something which you never felt so far.
It is a force,
Bountiful and ever merciful.

Look who I'm with-
Our grand father, our school teacher
All others who'd left us earlier!
There are more
Lot many our own people
Who came here before my birth.

Don't lament over
That mass I left behind.
Don't call it by my name-
For I can't be there within it
As for now-
I'm everywhere
Over the time and space.

# Quite Unusual

It was quite unusual
Since he would never request
For he had no great love for me-
Yet I did not think it important
When he wanted to see me
Being bedridden.

I heard about his general complaints though-
Of neglect and lack of care from near ones
Of ill health and uncertain future
And the stress of ageing.

I'm sure,
He didn't know either-
Future is never an extrapolation
Of the present state.

I left the place
Without meeting him
Even though I had wanted it.
Next time would be
More appropriate to see him

I thought-
When he would have recovered.

Now I feel
He didn't know
Beyond his consciousness
His body was sending some signals
We all failed to decode.

Only after a few hours
Someone broke me the news
That he's gone silent forever
Never needing any of the elements of the earth
That sustains life.

Now I realize-
Something was to leave soon
To be part of something else
There is a connection
Between where my imagination goes
And beyond
Above my ordinary comprehension.

# Surge of Memories

Like a storm surge on the quiet beach,
Like a glacial avalanche
Engulfing a sleepy hilly hamlet,
Like an eruption from a dead volcano
To the witness of a close visitor,
Like an earthquake of enormous intensity
During the most busy hour of the day
At times,
A gush of your memories and thoughts
Flood me
Making me stupefied:
I'm caught in a status
Of belief and disbelief,
In a moment of present and pleasant past,
In between pride and despair.

I come to senses
To find
The Tsunami of waves
Having left a trail of devastation
Where I rush
To collect the debris.

I gaze around for-
The so familiar voice and image
Till they escape my search
To appear again like a storm surge,
An avalanche,
An eruption
Or an earthquake later.

You are around for sure-
Or else how do I feel about you.

# Telepathy

Whenever a cloud of darkness
Hovers over my horizon
Or a strong breeze
Attempts to uproot me,
A slightest feeling of uneasiness
Or confounding thoughts
That leave me high and dry
Or at times while I am lost in the crowd
And despair to get out of it,
Then you ask-
If I'm not well
And what's gone wrong.

I would wonder-
How does one know
Not being around
When those others
Staying so near fail to know
When something goes wrong.

Someone said-
'Telepathy ' is it
And the basis of such feelings is
Nothing but love
Only love.

# The Convoluted Road

The road leads
Till the point it has been lighted
And much beyond.
She is in command.
My mind is a vehicle.

Silence is there
Though the souls are in dialogue.
There is no discomfort-
Only certain desires are heightened.

We have no destination.
We move through the circuitous road.
The thoughts and expressions run hither and thither
And convolute.

Soon we'll part our ways.
The chill of the night time will smother
The fire of the queries-
Not answered.
The night will be drenched in cold dews.
The mortal bodies will fall into sleep.

# The Fairy I Knew

No clue I had to know
Which place was that.
There're no signboards.
I had never been there before too.
How could I know the date?
I didn't recognise
Any single soul present around.

Yet I was there-
In a very beautiful garden
Bedecked with bright flowers of various colours
And laid on a carpet of grass.
On a sunny afternoon
A gentle and cool breeze soothing
The surroundings emitted an aura-
Of laughter, joy and lighter mood.

Seated as a beautiful damsel
Expressing a mesmerizing and soft chuckle,
Becoming a cynosure of everyone,
She noticed me yet
And I saw her too.

Surely the acquaintance got established-
She was the same girl
Gorgeous and striking as ever
Full of vigor, grace and charms.

Though she was  getting ready
For some event very important in her life,
But nothing prevented
As we were happily drifted together
To another space and time,
Much personal and intimate.

I didn't notice anyone there
Nor I remember anything we spoke
Though all I did see and feel
Boundless happiness and joy
Pouring down from everywhere.
The youthful emotions
Drenched our bodies, minds and souls

It is an eternal bliss
Flowing through
From thereon,
From a virtual realm
To my conscious existence.

# Till Infinity

How long will I be there?
Better you learn to grow up
And attend to the daily chores
Without my support.

To this poser
My little child
Who in an early phase of his life
Having seen blooming of life
And also the saddest moments
For certain losses,
With a glitter in his eyes-
As if he was the one
Who had seen the past and future
Replied 'infinity ' without any pause.

The answer left me
Nonplussed-
I will be there
Like I am here.

And the prompts came from within-
There is a lot of me in him.
Both would exist together
Like I'm an aggregate
Of all my forefathers
Who dropped their forms
And now constitute my subconscious.

# Unknown Fear

At this hour
Past midnight
No one is awoke
To communicate with-
The silence engulfs my neighborhood.
From a portion of my living space
Darkness is dispelled by the glowing lamps.
At times faint whispering sounds outside
Of wavering bamboo bushes rise
In a definite crescendo.
The infrequent falling of leaves
The occasional chirps of night birds
Make one feel certain difference.

Lo and behold
I think I can see
Being in clear senses-
You are here
Just in my front.
You don't speak.
You look angry
And bear no other expression

And you advance towards me
With a fury.
Almost tied to my bed
I'm helpless
As in no time
I will be finished
By the daggers you are holding
And I shout at my top
Seeking help to escape-
A certain death.

Later I realize-
In the company of family members
You couldn't have been there
For I'd seen your last journey
From all the living spaces
To the kingdom of void.
What then is the encounter that I had
In the night?
Was it created out of the fear
That I had from you
Which still hovers
Somewhere in my living space?

# Where are the Children Gone!

Where are the children gone!
The play fields are empty.
The elderly people aren't visible in the parks.
Few rodents run helter-skelter
In the hideouts the lovers'd prefer.

Few are seen buying and selling.
Deserted is the market place.
They seem in the grip of a fear uncertain.
No one is greeting, no one is smiling-
Another human may be carrying the virus.
From everywhere the usual crowd is gone.
Non-existent are all exchanges of emotions.

The roads in front of my house appear wide and long.
No vehicles are at sight.
The silence is eerie-
Seldom the sirens of ambulance puncturing it.

A great grief, panic and deep pain-
Seems looming all over.
The morning chants from the nearby temple are missing.
All are huddling in their havens.

We are aware of
All the ongoing human efforts.
Sooner those will yield results
As such a crisis isn't the first ever
The mankind faced.

Yet, without any effort
I kneel down-
Surrendering before all the might
Of unseen, all pervading being,
Pray with hope in the heart
We may be saved.

# Where is Her Brother?

Quietly I lined up
Behind her
As she started selecting
A rakhi,
Which she has been doing
Once in a year for years
To send to her brother living abroad
Which she did till last year.

She would pick up her choicest piece
Do some offerings to the God
Pray for the well being of her brother
Who in turn held promises
To give her all protection
Till the last breath.
She would expect a call
On the auspicious day
That her parcel was well received
And a photo with a Rakhi put on his wrist
Would complete the expectations of the day.

It has been a quiet ritual
Since they were brought up from being too small

Which built a relation
Of trust and love
Between a brother and a sister
As they grew up
Went to the school together
And got physically separated
Obeying the social norms.

After she bought few pieces
As she paid for those
She couldn't hold her tears
Since she didn't know
What to do this year
In which address to mail the Rakhi now.
As all addresses she knew
Had been erased
By the cruel hand of destiny.

It was not easy to see her sobbing
For she was in search
Of her young brother
While she knew for sure
He is not anywhere around
She could send her parcel
And confirm about its receipt
Like any other sister of India.

# Where is My King?

On this cold afternoon
By the seashore
The waves are crashing incessantly-
No sure if they forgot their rhythm.
Farther away
Another Sun was drowning-
Dousing of fire won't be easy.

All the shadows
Get bigger
To be merged ultimately
Within the veil of darkness.
The solitary bird has flapped away-
Much to my dismay
Inside the castle,
Gone silent.

There are stars.
There is moon in the sky.
The music of the night goes on.
Here I lie sleepless
Holding my unshed tears
And allowing to dry within-
Songs of my soul choke.

# Wounds

Nothing could be
Without a reason
Like my fresh wounds-
Where manifests a deep hatred
And a dreadful face mocks at me
From everywhere.
The guise of beauty is dropped.
All innocence were a cruel joke.
The hollow promises were veiled
To realize something selfishly.

At the same time-
The jewel like tear drops
In the eyes of the little one,
His silence,
Little care and touch
Fills up the empty
And wordless space
With divine bliss
And the pain goes away
Leaving the wound open
To heal on its own
In course of time.

He is too little.
How does he teach the elders
The price for the hatred
One should have to pay
When one of the biggest losses
Failed to teach someone!

The raison d'être is not yet over.
Few days will pass
Until the arrival of a new season
When certain compromises will be made
And normalcy will resume
Covering the unhealed scars.

Several layers of wounds lie
All unhealed
One over the other,
Not all could be from this life
Filling up the conscious
And unconscious mind
And haunting the living ones
Quietly from time to time.

# You must Come Out

We all believe-
You created us.
You are the source of life force.
All the non-living and living beings,
What we see, feel, smell and visualize
And things we can't comprehend too
Owe origin to You.

Human beings are-
Your best creations as
You made them as per Your own image.
Sages for countless number of years
Sat over meditations,
Adopted several means
To contemplate, comprehend and internalize
Your infinite and incomprehensible picture.

Like millions of humans, I believe
Nothing is possible if-
You were not the cause.
You exist here and there
Everywhere in everything.

Thousand years have passed-
You come out as deities every year
Of this temple so magnificent
And ride on a chariot most decorated
Along this grand pathway
Once to be with the devotees who love-
You as their creator- saviour
It's an ecstasy for several mortals
Who feel You from inside
And at Your momentary sight.

At this difficult time-
The whole of humanity is facing a test
And crying,
Immense are the people's sufferings,
The miseries are becoming limitless,
All the faiths too facing a crisis.

As an ardent devotee
I pray with all humilities at my command-
You must come out of the abode,
And see for Yourselves how
Your children are suffering.

It's another a thing-
If my faith is misplaced,
And the idols are simply man-made,
And the age old traditions are part of a social order
Under the control of few mortals!

# You are not a Whole Yourselves

Like the five elements
You are made of,
There is a bit of me in you.
You are not a whole yourself.

I think you are yet to know,
Who you are
And what you could do?
I had seen the sparks
When you were a child.

Before you were born
I was told about you
And a name had been given.
My garden then saw
Blooming of flowers
As if the earth was welcoming you
With a heavy shower of rains.

Often I saw
Purity in your thought,
Prayers in your mind,
And so much kindness in your heart.

When you saw an old woman
Begging in front of school
You wondered
"How does she survive
And if there was any one to take her care".
I had fumbled to explain
How God was taking her care
And who took away her hands.

As a small child
You'd courage to explain
The other little child crying
You were playing with
Whose castle of sand on the beach
Was washed away
By the mighty wave of the sea.
You'd consoled him
Assuring him to be back again together
To build more of those
As a rebuff to the cruel sea.

At times I saw you
Wiser than I was ever.
You could guide me
To be rightful when I faltered
Protected me when you thought
I needed love and care.

After I am gone
I wish to be there
In some bits of you.

If you love me
Look my dear
This is a world created by the God
Has offers many,
So much to live for
So much to wish for
So much to give and take.
Everything is possible
With His blessings.

# An Uncommon Guest

A forceful stream of cool breeze-
Originated all of a sudden
Just to bring along
A bouquet of fragrance
From over the rose garden.

I was drenched completely
As a pitcher of morning fresh dews burst
And it got drained out upon me
Quite unexpectedly.

It was not a dream-
That I was chasing.
I was shaken off nevertheless.
Though I felt being air borne
I held on to the ground
Under my feet.

I did simply follow
To where I was led.
The wings in the mind got power.
An uncommon guest that I was
In a beautiful kingdom.

Being still in senses
I couldn't believe-
How a mixture of dream and reality
Filled up my space!
The grace and youthful beauty
Infused blissful energy into the soul.

There was a whisper into my ear-
The life's lessons are simple,
Time runs out before you notice.
Few moments of love,
A fistful of happy memories
Make up the full worth of one's life.